It's MY Body

by Lory Freeman
illustrations Carol Deach

Lory Freeman is a preschool teacher for a Snohomish County Washington Co-operative Preschool. She is also the mother of two happy, satisfied children. She attended the University of California at Berkeley, and received both the Standard Elementary and the Early Childhood Teaching credentials from Sonoma State University in California.

Carol Deach is an award-winning Snohomish County Washington artist. She received her A.A. from Skagit Valley Junior College. She is the mother of two children, who served as models for the illustrations in It's MY Body.

Illustrations copyright © 1982 by Carol Deach
Text copyright © 1982 by Lory Freeman
First Printing: August 1983
Second Printing: March 1984
Third Printing: May 1984
Fourth Printing: August 1984
Fifth Printing: November 1984
Sixth Printing: March 1985

Parenting Press, Inc.

7750 31st Ave. NE Seattle, WA 98115

ISBN 0-943990-03-3 (paper)
ISBN 0-943990-02-5 (lib. bind.)

INTRODUCTION

It is important for parents and teachers to foster independence in young children by teaching effective means for coping with various situations. Theories of child development emphasize achieving autonomy through increased initiative and a sense of mastery.

Lory Freeman's book is consistent with these concepts, providing children an assertive stance for control of their own bodies and feelings. Her thoughtful approach prepares young children for appropriate responses to physical assault, and does so without provoking potentially damaging guilt feelings. *It's MY Body* is a sensitive way to introduce children to a prevalent problem in our culture.

Sondra Plone, Ph.D.
Psychology

Los Angeles, California
October, 1982

Dear Parents:

Until recently, sexual abuse was a crime rarely discussed with children. Most of us heard vague warnings about "strangers" from our parents, and we have, perhaps, relayed these warnings on to our children. However, few of us received any specific information about sexual abuse, or methods to use to protect ourselves. Thus, many conscientious parents hesitate to talk with their children about sexual abuse even though research has shown that children who have been informed about this crime are less likely to be victimized.

It's MY Body has been written in order to help adults and preschool children talk about sexual abuse together in a way which minimizes embarrassment and fear, but emphasizes self-reliance and open communication. You will not find specific references and stories about sexual abuse in this book. Preschool children are not ready for detailed discussions of this issue. They are ready, however, to learn how their feelings can help them make decisions about sharing their bodies, and how to communicate those decisions to others. This kind of learning serves as a vital first step in the protection of children from sexual abuse.

Thus we encourage you not to just read this book **to** your children, but to **share** the book together. As you read the text, ask your children to share their thoughts and feelings about different kinds of touch. Try to remember back to your childhood and recapture your childhood feelings about sharing your body. You may wish to tell your children about some of these experiences.

It's MY Body teaches children two "touching codes" which should become automatic responses to uncomfortable touch situations. This protective strategy for your children can be introduced by having them practice the codes with you as you read *It's MY Body.* Coach your children to look you in the eye, to hold up their hands, and to say the codes without giggling — like they "really mean it".

Once your children have learned these codes, you can reinforce their understanding by telling situation stories which involve the use of a touching code. For example, the touching code is an appropriate response to an unwanted hug, uncomfortable tickling or wrestling.

When you have finished reading *It's MY Body* and talking about the touching codes, be sure to tell your children that if they are touched by anyone in a way that makes them feel uncomfortable, to come and tell you right away.

Most children like *IT'S MY Body* so much they want to hear it read over and over. This is well, as preventative safety teaching must be repeated often until children have truly absorbed the protective strategies.

It's MY Body provides parents with a positive, self-affirming method of protective teaching. We hope that you and your children will find sharing this book to be an enjoyable, growing experience.

Janie Hart-Rossi

Janie Hart-Rossi
Sexual Abuse Prevention Educator

I have something very special
that belongs to only me.

I was born with it . . .

And it changes as I grow older.

But it is always just mine!
It's my body.

Sometimes I like to share my body . . .

When I hug my father,
I am sharing my body.

When I sit on my grandma's lap,
I am sharing my body.

When I hold a little baby's hand,
I am sharing my body.

When I let someone tickle me,
I am sharing my body.

Even when I am sharing my body,
it is always something special that
belongs only to me.

Sometimes I don't like to share my body.

If someone is tickling me too hard,
I might not feel like sharing my body.

If someone wants to give me a big slurpy kiss, I might not feel like sharing my body.

If a dog is licking me, I might not
want to share my body with the dog.

If **someone** is holding me too tightly,
I might not feel like sharing my body.

If someone wants to touch me any place
or way that makes me feel uncomfortable,
I won't share my body!

This is what I say:

"Don't touch me! I don't like it!"

If someone wants me to touch them
any place or way that makes me feel
uncomfortable, I won't share my body!

This is what I say:
"No, I won't touch you. I don't like it!"

Now YOU practice saying it loud and clear.
"Don't touch me! I don't like it!"

and . . .
"No, I won't touch you! I don't like it!"

You will probably feel warm inside when you
share your body because you want to.

But, if you feel uncomfortable inside,
  don't share your body!

Remember . . .
Your body is something very special
that belongs only to you!